KEEP YOUR EYE ON THE KID

To the memory of those who made us laugh: the motley mountebanks, the clowns, the buffoons, in all times and in all nations, whose efforts have lightened our burden a little, this picture [book] is affectionately dedicated.

—Preston Sturges, *Sullivan's Travels*

I was born in a rooming house midway between the church and the railroad in Piqua, Kansas. My folks were traveling show people.

I was a backstage baby. I sat on frogs' knees and I talked to wooden dummies while Dad and Mom did their act. They were called The Keatons, and I was Joe Keaton, like my dad.

Then, one morning when I was fooling around, I took a tumble. Harry Houdini picked me up and gave me my new name. You had to know how to take a fall in our business.

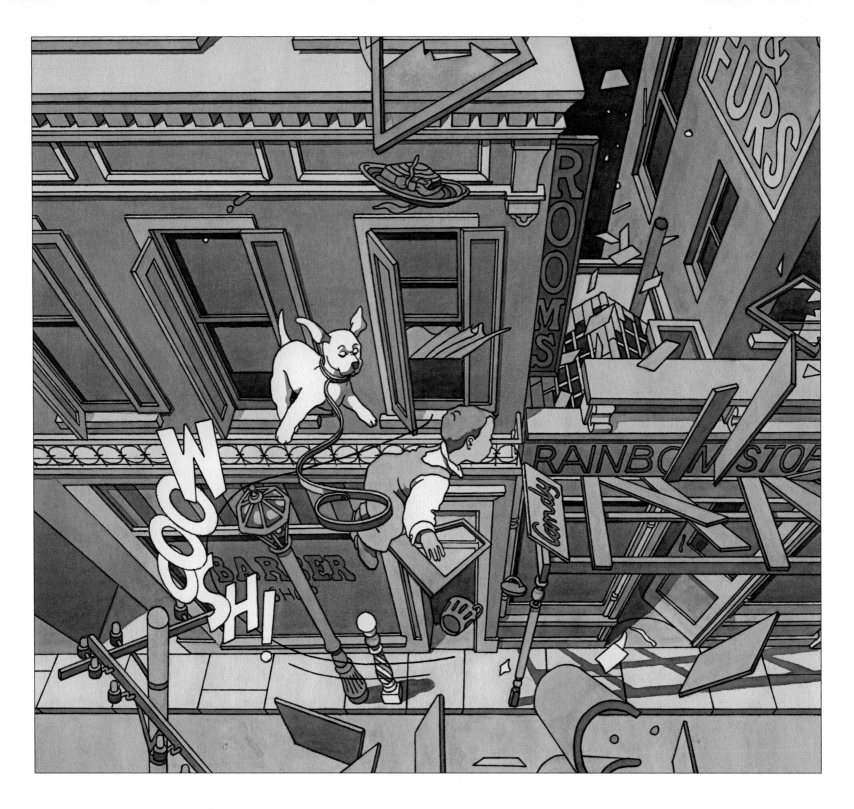

And you had to be lucky, like the night I went flying. They say I got sucked out of the window by a tornado.

I landed right there on Main Street, without a scratch. Boy, was Dad proud of me.

On the night I broke into the act, Dad threw me across the stage shouting, "Keep your eye on the kid!" and the crowd went crazy.

Folks liked me better when I didn't smile.
Dad would hiss, "Face!" at me, and they all cheered. That's the way it went, all across America.

We worked at night, and by day there was always some guy to teach me how to soft-shoe shuffle or tell me wild stories.

I saw more of America when I was a kid than most folks do in their lifetimes.

As for school, I went only one day. Miss What's-Her-Name said, "You, Keaton, give me a sentence with the word *delight*." Without thinking, I said, "It's dark, turn on delight." Yep, I got expelled for wisecracking, and that was it. I never went back. Ever.

But I learned things. In the long afternoons before the show, I'd clear off on my own. One day I saw folks waiting to go into a store. It had a sign saying "Moving Pictures 1 Hour for 5¢."

I followed them in. It was dark. And there, up on a sheet, was a big moving picture of the sea. I had never seen the sea.

Then a train came straight out at us. Did those folks jump! Not me, though. I just wanted to know how it was done.

I asked the guy in the storeroom out back. "Well, kid," he said, "this here's the projector, the film goes in here." That kind of thing.

I was hooked. As I grew up, every chance I got I went to the movies.

Dad hated the movies. He got real mad at me, and we fought about it until I was too big for him to throw. So I packed my bags and headed for New York.

I was looking for work. Then on the street, I met my vaudeville pal Roscoe Arbuckle! He told me he was in movies. He took me to his studio.

Roscoe was real good to me. I met his movie pals and they explained things, showed me how the studio worked. I'd never seen a camera close up before, so Roscoe said, "Go on, kid, take it home and check it out."

That night I took it apart and then I put it back together again. Gee, that thing, I loved it. Just the feel of it.

Next day, I acted in a movie for the very first time. It was *The Butcher Boy*. Roscoe knew the Three Keatons act. He knew I could take a fall. Did we have fun!

Not long after, we all headed for California. Long sunny days for shooting films. Now I am making my own movies. Joe Schenck gave me my own studio.

I have a gang of guys I work with. I'm boss, but we all pitch in with ideas for gags. We plan it, we build it…

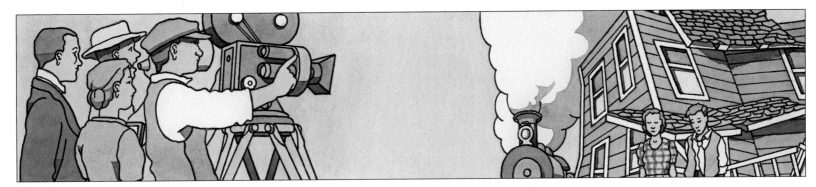

... then we shoot it.

We plan it, we build it…

… then we shoot it.

I'm making my name making movies.
Even Dad has joined me. He's going around telling everyone movies are here to stay.
I'm thinking I told him that some time ago.

BUSTER KEATON

Buster Keaton was born in 1895 in Piqua, Kansas, where his parents were performing in the Mohawk Indian Medicine Show. His childhood was spent traveling across the States from one performance to another. The Keatons kept moving to avoid the Gerry Society, which worked to enforce child-labor laws. No child under the age of seven was permitted to even walk on stage, but Buster was part of the act from the age of three.

His story has been recounted so many times that it is often impossible to separate the facts from the fiction. Buster himself told a good story, including the one about being sucked out of a window by a tornado. Another favorite story describes his father's response to an official inquiring about Buster's age (Buster was dressed in a suit and tie). It is said that Joe Keaton shrugged and pointed to Buster's mother: "I don't know, ask his wife."

Buster acquired his agility and comic timing from working with show people and vaudeville performers, so when he encountered Roscoe "Fatty" Arbuckle in New York, it was a stroke of luck. Arbuckle had been a vaudevillian and had no hesitation in taking the young Buster under his wing. He was making low-budget movies in a studio where everyone contributed—the cameraman helped build the set, the set builder fixed the lighting, the storyline and gags would change as ideas were bounced around, and most of the crew appeared in front of the camera when required. Buster fitted into this work pattern with ease. It was the way he loved to work, and it was here that he learned skills that he later used in his own films.

Joseph Schenck was Arbuckle's producer and when the studio relocated to California, Schenck funded Buster's movies. Buster developed a style that combined the clowning and stone face of his childhood with the visual tricks that became his trademark. While others overacted for the silent screen, Buster underplayed. He planned and carried out his gags with a grace and agility that leave the audience gasping. He is perhaps best known for the much-admired gag of the falling wall in *Steamboat Bill, Jr.* (shown on the previous page), which still takes my breath away every time I see it.

Buster made his best work in a mere ten years. His most famous films include my favorite, *One Week* (1920), where a train smashed through Buster's misconstructed house, *Our Hospitality* (1923), *The Navigator* (1924), *The General* (1926), and *Steamboat Bill, Jr.* (1928).

SOME SOURCES

Rudi Blesh, *Keaton*. New York: Macmillan, 1966.

Kevin Brownlow, *Hollywood: The Pioneers*. New York: Alfred A. Knopf, 1979.

Buster Keaton and Charles Samuels, *My Wonderful World of Slapstick*. New York: DaCapo Press, 1982.

Eleanor Keaton, *Buster Keaton Remembered*. New York: Harry N. Abrams, 2001.

Martin W. Sandler, *This Was America*. Boston: Little, Brown & Company, 1980.

SOME FILMS

John G. Blystone and Buster Keaton, *Our Hospitality/Sherlock, Jr.* Joseph M. Schenck Productions, 1923. DVD.

Clyde Bruckman and Buster Keaton, *The General*. Buster Keaton Productions, Inc., 1927. DVD.

Donald Crisp and Buster Keaton, *The Navigator*. Buster Keaton Productions, Inc., 1924. DVD.

Chas. F. Reisner, *Steamboat Bill, Jr.* Buster Keaton Productions, Inc., 1928. DVD.

Text and illustrations copyright © 2008 by Catherine Brighton
Page 32 photo courtesy the Library of Congress, Prints and Photographs Division

Flash Point is an imprint of Roaring Brook Press, a division of Holtzbrinck Publishing Holdings Limited Partnership
175 Fifth Avenue, New York, NY 10010

Distributed in Canada by H. B. Fenn and Company Ltd.

Library of Congress Cataloging-in-Publication Data:
Brighton, Catherine.
Keep your eye on the kid : the early years of Buster Keaton / Catherine Brighton. — 1st ed.
p. cm.
Includes bibliographical references.
ISBN-13: 978-1-59643-158-4
ISBN-10: 1-59643-158-X
1. Keaton, Buster, 1895–1966—Childhood and youth—Juvenile literature. 2. Motion picture actors and actresses—United States—Biography—Juvenile literature. I. Title.
PN2287.K4B75 2008   791.4302'8092—dc22
[B]   2007016534

Roaring Brook Press books are available for special promotions and premiums.
For details contact: Director of Special Markets, Holtzbrinck Publishers.

First Edition April 2008
Book design by Mary Ellen Casey
Cover design by Alex Ferrari

Printed in China
1 3 5 7 9 10 8 6 4 2